MAJOR WORLD RELIGIONS

Christianity

Major World Religions

Buddhism

Christianity

Hinduism

Islam

Judaism

Sikhism

MAJOR WORLD RELIGIONS

Christianity

Aaron Bowen

MC MASON CREST
PHILADELPHIA

Mason Crest
450 Parkway Drive, Suite D
Broomall, PA 19008
www.masoncrest.com

©2018 by Mason Crest, an imprint of National Highlights, Inc.

Printed and bound in the United States of America.

CPSIA Compliance Information: Batch #MWR2017.
For further information, contact Mason Crest at 1-866-MCP-Book.

3 5 7 9 8 6 4 2

Library of Congress Cataloging-in-Publication Data

on file at the Library of Congress
ISBN: 978-1-4222-3817-2 (hc)
ISBN: 978-1-4222-7970-0 (ebook)

Major World Religions series ISBN: 978-1-4222-3815-8

QR CODES AND LINKS TO THIRD-PARTY CONTENT

Table of Contents

KEY ICONS TO LOOK FOR:

Words to understand: These words with their easy-to-understand definitions will increase the reader's understanding of the text while building vocabulary skills.

Sidebars: This boxed material within the main text allows readers to build knowledge, gain insights, explore possibilities, and broaden their perspectives by weaving together additional information to provide realistic and holistic perspectives.

Educational Videos: Readers can view videos by scanning our QR codes, providing them with additional educational content to supplement the text. Examples include news coverage, moments in history, speeches, iconic sports moments and much more!

Text-dependent questions: These questions send the reader back to the text for more careful attention to the evidence presented there.

Research projects: Readers are pointed toward areas of further inquiry connected to each chapter. Suggestions are provided for projects that encourage deeper research and analysis.

Series glossary of key terms: This back-of-the book glossary contains terminology used throughout this series. Words found here increase the reader's ability to read and comprehend higher-level books and articles in this field.

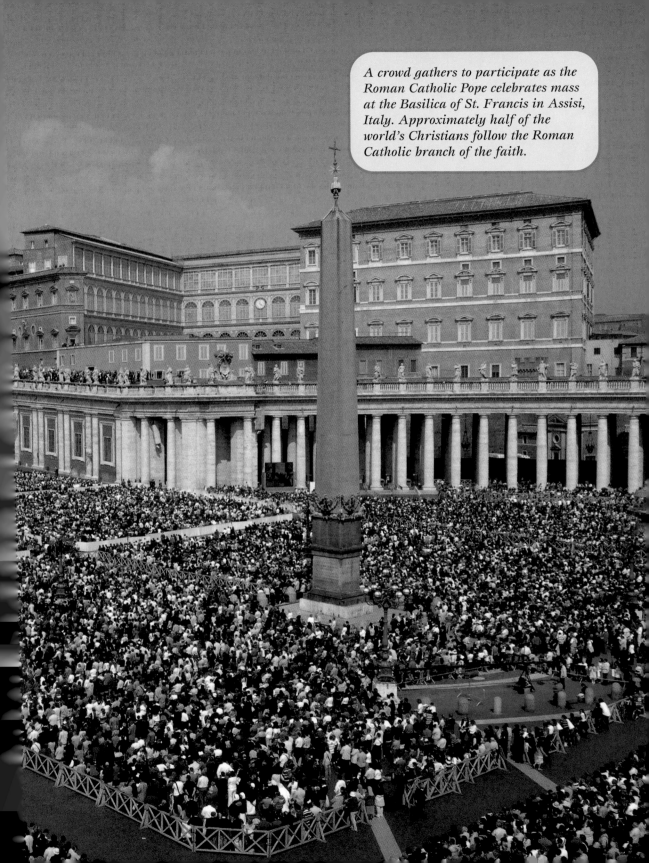

A crowd gathers to participate as the Roman Catholic Pope celebrates mass at the Basilica of St. Francis in Assisi, Italy. Approximately half of the world's Christians follow the Roman Catholic branch of the faith.

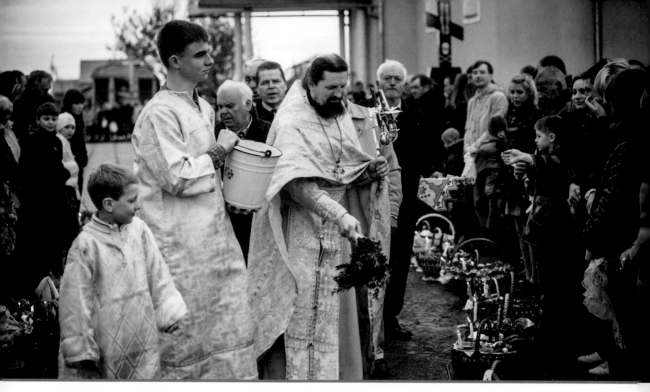

 # Words to Understand in This Chapter

blasphemy—disrespectful talk about God or sacred things.

disciple—someone who followed Jesus during his life. A follower or pupil of a teacher.

Gospel—meaning 'Good news'. One of the four books in the Bible that tell us about Jesus's life.

Messiah—the long awaited Anointed One of God who would right all wrongs and bring about the Kingdom, or rule, of God on Earth.

miracle—an extraordinary and welcome event that cannot be explained by the laws of nature or science.

parables—stories with levels of meanings used to make a point. A lot of Jesus's teaching took the form of parables.

resurrection—Jesus's rising from the dead.

sin—going against God's wishes. Something separating a person from God.

soul—the spiritual part of a person.

testament—another word for "promise." The Bible consists of the Old Testament (the laws of Moses and the witness of the Jewish prophets) and the New Testament (the witness of Jesus's life and times).

An Orthodox priest blesses baskets of eggs, bread, and sweets that are given to those participating in an Easter morning service in Ukraine. The death and resurrection of Jesus Christ, through which he paid for the sins of humanity, is the most important belief held by Christians.

1 What Do Christians Believe?

Christians believe in the teachings of Jesus Christ. Jesus was a teacher and preacher who grew up more than 2,000 years ago in Galilee, a region that is now part of Israel. Jesus said he had come to teach the true meaning of the religious teachings of the Jews. These teachings had been given to the Jewish people over many centuries.

Jesus taught that all the rules and teachings about how to live could be summed up in a few short sentences. First, Jesus said, was for believers to acknowledge that, "God is the only Lord. Love the Lord your God with all your heart, with all your *soul*, with all your mind, and with all your strength." His second most important message was, "Love your neighbor as you love yourself."

An Influential Teacher

Jesus tried to show people how important it was to follow God's teachings. He asked people to accept God into their lives. He taught using captivating stories that had layers of meaning, called *parables*. A parable can be simply enjoyed and remembered as a good story, easily memorized for

 ## Teaching With Parables

Parables were a form of teaching used by the Jews of Jesus's time. Jewish rabbis, or spiritual leaders, used stories from everyday life to entertain and teach. The following is one of Jesus's parables:

"The kingdom of God is like a mustard seed, which a man took and sowed in his field. As a seed, mustard is smaller than any other; but when it has grown, it is bigger than any garden-plant; it becomes a tree, big enough for birds to come and roost among its branches."

Some people interpret the parable to be about the growth of Christianity. Jesus is the man who sowed the seed in his field. Mustard seeds are very small, but they produce large plants that grow quickly and soon take over most of the field. The Christian church that Jesus established also started out small, but grew relatively quickly. Today, Christianity is the world's largest religion with more than 2.2 billion followers.

Jesus told his followers to pray in this way: "Our Father, who art in heaven, hallowed be thy name. Thy kingdom come, thy will be done, on Earth as it is in Heaven. Give us this day our daily bread. Forgive us the wrong we have done, as we have forgiven those who have wronged us. And do not bring us to the test, but deliver us from evil."

retelling or thinking about later. Jesus's parables encouraged listeners to think of new interpretations as their faith grew. Some parables were long stories, others were just a few sentences long. Almost all of them were taken from everyday situations that the people living at the time would have been able to relate to. They gave meaning to people's lives.

Jesus also used *miracles* to teach. Miracles were not new in the Jewish tradition; they were signs of the power of God.

There are stories about Jesus quieting a storm when his *disciples* were afraid and of healing a paralyzed man after telling him his *sins* were forgiven.

Jesus used miracles as a demonstration of God's power. There have been many healers before, during and since Jesus's time. Today many Christians claim to use the power of Jesus to heal, and some people do seem to have been healed. What Jesus claimed was that he had the power to forgive sins. Some of his healings imply that the person's illness was caused by the sinful acts of that person. So by curing the illness, Jesus was forgiving the person's sins. The Jewish authorities, however, believed Jesus's claim was

What Does "Church" Mean?

Christians use the word "church" in four main ways. It can mean the building in which Christians meet to worship. It can refer to the people who worship in that building—the congregation. The word "Church" can also mean the members of a specific branch of Christianity, such as the Roman Catholic Church or the Methodist Church. There are three main branches of Christianity—Roman Catholic, Eastern Orthodox, and Protestant churches. Churches with slightly different beliefs within one of these branches are called denominations—for example, Lutherans and Methodists are Protestant denominations. The word "Church" can also be used to refer to the entire community of Christians throughout the world.

blasphemy, punishable by death, because only God could forgive sins.

Jesus did not heal people only out of compassion or pity. He may have cured only a small percentage of sick or disabled people living around him. Jesus healed to speak about himself and the power of God. People had to understand who and what Jesus was. Jesus healed blind people and deaf people as a sign that those who listened to him would see and hear what he taught. "Look," "listen," and "understand" are important words in the *Gospel* stories of Jesus.

Educational Video

Scan here to see a short video on one of Jesus's well-known parables:

A Saving Message

The Jewish religious authorities did not approve of Jesus's teachings. He was seen as a threat to the community, and was sentenced to death. Christians believe that three days after he was crucified, Jesus rose from the dead and is alive today. This makes the life of Jesus very special.

For Christians, the most special events of Jesus's life were his birth, death and *resurrection*. They believe that God sent his only son, Jesus, to share in what it means to be a human being. Jesus was so obedient to God's wishes that he was prepared to die an agonizing death. Because he did what God asked he rose from the dead and others who followed him would also live forever with God in heaven.

Most Christians believe that Jesus rising from the dead is literally true—a historical fact. Others believe it is a way of describing how powerfully his followers felt him to be with them after his death.

Christians believe there is, and only ever has been, one God. However, they refer to God in three ways: as the Father Creator; as the Son, Jesus Christ; and as the Holy Spirit, the power of God that people feel and experience in their lives. So Christians talk about God as Father, Son and Holy Spirit, or the Trinity—three in one. For Christians, the idea of Father, Son and Holy Spirit expresses the principal ways God and human beings interact with each other.

Christianity is a religion of salvation—deliverance from the power and effects of sin. It teaches that human beings

Christ, the Messiah

Christians believe that Jesus was the Christ. The word "Christ" comes from a Greek word, *christos*, which, in turn, is a translation of the Hebrew word *mosaich*, or **Messiah**, which means "Anointed One" or "Chosen One." The Jews believe that the Messiah, a leader chosen by God, will come one day to bring about the rule of God on Earth. It will be a time of justice, peace and harmony. There are many prophecies about the Messiah in the Jewish scriptures. Christians believe that Jesus is the Anointed One promised by God. So the name Jesus Christ means "Jesus the Messiah."

have disobeyed the commands God gave to the Jewish people. In breaking these laws, people became separated from God. Christians believe that Jesus's life and death mended that relationship. Those who listened to Jesus's teaching and believed in him would enter into a new and special relationship with God. Their wrongdoings, or sins, would be forgiven and they would be reunited with God in heaven.

 Text-Dependent Questions

1. What two statements did Jesus say summed up all the rules and teachings for how to live?
2. What is a parable?
3. What is the Trinity?

 Research Project

Using the Internet or your school library, do some research to answer the question "Do religious believers need a special place of worship?" Those who agree will say that believers should be allowed to give God their very best, whatever it costs. The design of the building can create a setting that helps people to worship. Those who disagree with this perspective believe that it is not right to spend money on places of worship when people are starving all over the world. Moreover, they contend, if God is everywhere, what need is there for special places of worship? Present your conclusion in a two-page report, providing examples from your research that support your answer.

 Words to Understand in This Chapter

ascend—to go up, or rise.

baptism—a ceremony through which a person joins the Christian Church. It involves the sprinkling or pouring of water on to a person's forehead or immersing the whole body in water.

ministry—work with, and spiritual service to, other people.

prophet—someone who speaks for God and tells people what God wants.

sacrifice—give up something precious, including one's own life.

synagogue—a building where Jewish people meet, pray and study.

Stained glass windows and illustrations, like this one from the chapel of the Swiss guards in Vatican City, often tell Bible stories because for many centuries few people could read. Here, Jesus meets with some of his female disciples while he is carrying the cross to Calvary. Despite his own suffering, he takes time to comfort them.

2 The Life of Jesus

hristianity originated as a sect of Judaism, a set of religious and cultural beliefs that originated in the Middle East around 4,000 years ago. The ancestors of the Jewish people, known as Israelites or Hebrews, believed that God, the creator of the universe, had chosen them to be His special people. Unlike most of the other tribal groups in the Middle East at the time, the Jews only worshiped one God, whom they called YHWH (an unpronounceable word in the Jewish language, because God's name is so holy it cannot be spoken) or Adonai ("Lord").

The Jewish Religion

God gave the Hebrews a series of laws and commandments to follow. These were given to a leader named Moses on Mount Sinai, as the people were fleeing from slavery in

Egypt around the year 1500 BCE. The Hebrews eventually settled in the region that today is the State of Israel, with the city of Jerusalem as their capital. Jerusalem was home to an important temple, where *sacrifices* were made to God as spelled out in the laws that Moses provided. These laws are included in the Torah, five sacred books that Jews believe were written by Moses. The books also tell stories about the creation of the world by God, and about the ancestors of the Hebrews. These included Adam and Eve, the first man and woman; Noah, who saved humanity from a worldwide flood; Abraham, with whom God established his covenant; and Abraham's son Isaac, grandson Jacob, and great-grandson Joseph, through whom God continued to bless the Hebrews.

The most important of the laws given to Moses are known as the Ten Commandments. They form the basis of Jewish law, and have had a huge influence on modern Western values and culture. The commandments emphasize that there is only one God, and that only He must be worshiped. They also prohibit such actions as theft, murder, adultery, lying, and swearing, and jealousy.

Moses led the Hebrews to a region called Canaan, which roughly corresponds to the modern states of Israel and Jordan. Over a long period of time, the Hebrews conquered the more sophisticated Canaanite civilization and established their own kingdom of Israel.

During the reign of King David (1000–961 BCE), Israel achieved its greatest glory. David captured the city of Jerusalem and made it his capital. David's kingdom covered

The Ten Commandments

The Ten Commandments are the basis of Jewish Law, and are listed twice in the Old Testament, in the books of Exodus and Deuteronomy. Although both Jews and Christians consider these books to be sacred, they differ on exactly how the commandments are numbered. The Roman Catholic numbering of the ten commandments is as follows:

1. I am the Lord your God, who brought you out of the land of Egypt. You shall have no other gods before me.
2. You shall not make for yourself graven images, or bow down to idols or serve them.
3. You shall not take the name of the Lord your God in vain.
4. Remember the Sabbath day, to keep it holy. Six days you shall labor and do all your work, but the seventh day is the Sabbath to the Lord your God; on it you shall not do any work.
5. Honor your father and mother.
6. You shall not kill.
7. You shall not commit adultery.
8. You shall not steal.
9. You shall not bear false witness against your neighbor.
10. You shall not covet your neighbor's goods or wife.

Statue of Moses holding the stone tablets that contain God's law. Moses is revered by Jews and Christians as a great emancipator and lawgiver.

the area of the modern-day state of Israel, as well as parts of Lebanon, Syria, Jordan, and Iraq. This was a time in ancient history when the traditional world powers of the Middle East—empires based in Mesopotamia and Egypt—were comparatively weak. As a result Israel, which controlled the trade routes between these two empires, emerged as major power of the time.

David's son Solomon was considered a wise ruler who maintained the strong position of Israel. Solomon is also credited with building an enormous Holy Temple in Jerusalem where God could be worshiped. However, after Solomon's death around 922 BCE, the kingdom became divided. The kingdom of Judah was established in the southern part of the country, including Jerusalem. The kingdom of Israel controlled the northern regions and was also known as the Northern Kingdom. Its capital was the city of Samaria.

The Fall of Israel, and Exile

In 722 BCE the Northern Kingdom was conquered by the powerful Assyrians, and the people who lived there were dispersed to other lands. In 586 BCE the Babylonians conquered Judah, capturing Jerusalem and destroying the Holy Temple. Many of the Israelites were taken as prisoners to Babylon.

Over the next 600 years, the Israelites' religion underwent significant changes. With the Temple—the focal point of the Israelite religion—destroyed, *prophets* appeared to explain that no matter where the people were, they could establish a relationship with God on an individual and personal basis. It was at this point that the religion began to be referred to as Judaism, and the people who practiced it as Jews.

The exile forced the Israelites to reconsider their view of God. In the past, they had worshiped God while at the same time considering the deities of other nations legitimate—and sometimes even worshipping other gods as well. In Babylon, the Jewish prophets taught that God controlled all of history, and that there were no other gods or forces that could affect their lives. The prophets taught that if the Israelites obeyed the laws that God had given them through Moses, then God would save them from captivity and one day

David was an effective king of Israel. In exile, the Jews came to believe that the Messiah would be his descendant.

He would establish a new kingdom that would be greater than King David's.

Eventually, the Babylonians were themselves conquered by the Persians, and Jews were permitted to return to Jerusalem. However, for most of the next six centuries they would continue to be ruled by other empires: first the Persians from 539 to 334 BCE; then the Greeks from 334 until about 164 BCE. Jews won independence from the Greeks in the Maccabean Revolt, and maintained a small kingdom, known as Judea, for about a hundred years. The Roman Empire gained control over Judea by 64 BCE.

Throughout this time, Jews waited for God to establish the new Jewish state. Many Jewish prophets—from Isaiah, who lived at the time of the Babylonian exile, to Daniel, whose writings dated to the end of the Persian period—had predicted that one day a great leader from the line of King David would come and establish a kingdom even greater than ancient Israel. This priest-king would be the *moshiach*, or Messiah—the savior of the Jews.

The Life of Jesus

Somewhere around the year 4 BCE, while Judea languished as a Roman province, a child was born to a Jewish couple in the small town of Bethlehem. His parents named him Yeshua, which in Hebrew means "to deliver" or "to rescue." He is known today by the Greek form of this name: Jesus.

According to Christian writings about the life of Jesus, unusual signs and miracles occurred at his birth. These

This painting of the birth of Jesus, or nativity, was done by Pietro Dufour in 1689; it is displayed in a church in Turin, Italy.

The New Testament says that God chose a young unmarried woman named Mary to be the mother of Jesus. Roman Catholics have a special veneration for Mary, believing that she can intercede with Jesus to grant requests. Other Christians do not share this belief, preferring to direct their prayers directly to Jesus.

included a visit from heavenly angels, as well as a star that appeared in the sky over the place where he was born. The star attracted the attention of wise men from Persia, who interpreted this as a sign that a great new king had been born. They journeyed for a long time with gifts to welcome the king.

Jesus was a Jew like his parents, and he grew up in a town called Nazareth, in the area around the Sea of Galilee, a large lake in northern Israel. It is said that his father, a carpenter, was a descendant of King David.

Very little is known about Jesus's early life. When he was about 30 years old, he was *baptized* in the Jordan River by a man named John the Baptist. John was a cousin of Jesus's who had been living in the wilderness, encouraging the Jews to repent of sinful behavior. John baptized people in the river as a way for them to symbolically re-dedicate their lives to worshipping God.

Jesus soon began to preach a message of reform and repentance in Jewish communities throughout the Galilee region. He emphasized the importance of obeying God's law, but encouraged Jews to focus on spiritual matters and the glorification of God. Wherever he went, Jesus healed sick people and performed miracles to show the power of God. He soon gathered a group of followers, known as disciples. Among them were his twelve closest followers, who were called apostles.

Because Jesus was a Jew, he often taught in the *synagogues* of towns that he visited. His teaching followed a traditional Jewish style of religious discussion, and he often quoted from the Jewish scriptures to make important points. Some Jews heard what Jesus had to say and embraced his message. Others were offended by his teach-

This ancient mosaic from a church in modern-day Bosnia and Herzegovina shows John the Baptist pouring water on the head of Jesus.

ings, which they believed were sacrilegious—particularly his claim to be the Son of God.

Understanding Jesus's Teachings

The apostles and disciples believed that Jesus was the Messiah that the prophets had foretold. However, according to the Gospels, they misunderstood Jesus's teaching. They believed he had come to free the Jews from Roman rule and establish a kingdom on Earth. Instead, Jesus explained, he was the Son of God and had come to save all of humanity from its sins.

These statues of Jesus instructing the Twelve Apostles are located near the Sea of Galilee, not far from the spot where Jesus is believed to have taught a crowd of people in a famous discourse known as the Sermon on the Mount.

The Jewish tradition taught that humans had sinned since the time of Adam. Jews believed that when they violated the laws of Moses, their sins could be forgiven if they participated in certain rituals of atonement. Jesus argued that many Jews placed too much emphasis on carefully following the rituals, and not enough time truly repenting of their sins and reflecting on how God wanted His people to live. Jesus taught that God was angered by pride, but pleased by humble penitence and service to others.

Jesus said that the Jews still had to observe the laws of Moses, but he also insisted that the spirit of those laws be followed. The Ten Commandments forbade people from committing adultery—but Jesus said that anyone who even thought about committing adultery was guilty of violating the law. Jesus told his followers to love their enemies, and pray for those who persecuted them. He told them not to fight back when attacked, and to share what they had with others.

Holy Week

In the four Gospels, the last week of Jesus's life is given the greatest importance. For Christians, the events of this week are the fulfillment of centuries of Jewish prophesy.

According to the Gospels, Jesus taught in the communities around the Sea of Galilee for about three years. When he was thirty-three years old, around the year 29 CE, Jesus and his followers traveled to Jerusalem to celebrate a Jewish holiday known as Passover. This holiday was one of the most important festivals of the Jewish calendar, occurring

A Nicaraguan priest leads his congregation in a Palm Sunday parade. Palm Sunday marks the start of Holy Week, and commemorates Jesus's arrival at Jerusalem.

in the springtime. Passover commemorates an incident when the Hebrew people were captives in Egypt during the time of Moses, when God sent the Angel of Death to kill all of the firstborn children. The Angel "passed over" the homes of the Hebrews, but devastated the Egyptians—an event that drove the Pharaoh to allow the Hebrew slaves to leave Egypt.

Crowds of people welcomed Jesus as he arrived in Jerusalem. They had heard about the miracles he had performed, and many of them probably thought he was coming to start a revolution against the Roman authorities. The Gospels say that people in the crowds waved palm branches, throwing them before Jesus and shouting, "Praise to the Son of David! Blessings on him who comes in the name of the Lord!" The palm branches were a symbol from the coins when Judea was an independent kingdom; calling Jesus the "Son of David" was a reference to him as the successor to Israel's greatest king.

Jesus arrived at the city riding on a donkey. This fulfilled a Jewish prophesy that the Messiah would come to Jerusalem on a beast of burden. To enter Jerusalem on a horse would resemble a conquering king; to enter on a donkey was a symbol of humility.

Every year, thousands of Jews came to Jerusalem for the Passover festival. The Roman authorities always prepared for disturbances by sending more soldiers to the city. In previous years there had been Jewish revolts that had to be quelled by arresting and executing the leaders.

During the first few days he was in Jerusalem, Jesus taught at the Temple. He made a scene one day when he drove out merchants who were doing business inside the Temple, which Jesus felt was inappropriate in a place dedicated to worshipping God. He also criticized two groups of Jewish leaders, the Pharisees and the Saducees, for putting too much emphasis on tradition and not enough on true repentance.

The Jewish leaders disagreed with Jesus's teachings and were offended that he claimed to be the Son of God. Members of the Sanhedrin, a group of 70 leaders of the

Jewish community in Jerusalem, collaborated with Roman authorities, requesting that they arrest Jesus as a threat to Rome.

The Passion

Jesus celebrated Passover by eating a meal with the Twelve Apostles. During the meal, Jesus asked his apostles to remember him and his teachings every time that they broke bread and drank wine together in the future, saying, "Do this in remembrance of me." Jesus also told them that one of the apostles who was sharing the meal would betray him to the authorities, and that Peter, the leading apostle, would deny knowing him three times that very night. The meal is known as the Last Supper.

Afterward, Jesus asked three of his apostles—Peter, John, and James—to come with him to a quiet garden near Jerusalem, where he could pray. While they were there, Roman soldiers arrived to arrest Jesus. They were brought there by Judas, one of the apostles. Judas was a zealot, a member of a Jewish group that wanted to overthrow Roman rule. Judas had been paid off by the Jewish authorities to betray Jesus, but he may also have believed that Jesus would use his power to destroy the arresting Roman soldiers and start the revolution that would drive out the Romans. Instead, however, Jesus submitted to arrest without resisting.

During the night, Jesus was placed on trial before the Jewish authorities, as well as before a Roman ruler named Pontius Pilate. The Gospels say that Pilate did not find

This artwork from a Croatian church shows Jesus being led away after being condemned to death. The Roman leader Pontius Pilate is pictured at right. The Bible indicates that Pilate was reluctant to order Jesus's execution. However, because Jesus was accused of leading a political insurgency, Pilate's loyalty to the Roman empire might have been questioned if he had shown mercy. The Gospel of Matthew notes that Pilate washed his hands after the sentencing, symbolically indicating to the Jewish crowd that he would not take responsibility for the crucifixion of Jesus.

In Roman times, to be crucified meant more than that a crime worthy of death had been committed. It also meant that the accused was considered to be a lowly, vile, reprehensible person, in addition to being a criminal.

Jesus to be guilty of any wrongdoing. Despite this, Pilate ordered that Jesus be tortured and executed.

Jesus was flogged and humiliated, then forced to carry a heavy, wooden cross through the streets of Jerusalem. When he reached the top of a high place outside the city known as Calvary, his hands and feet were nailed to the cross, and he was left to die.

Crucifixion was a common Roman method used to kill criminals. Thousands of people were crucified each year, and Jesus himself was hung between two thieves. It was a brutal way for someone to die, as they suffered intense pain and eventually died from blood loss and exposure. It could take a day or more for someone to die, but the Romans sometimes expedited the process by smashing the legs of criminals with a heavy sledgehammer, so that the crucified person could no longer hold himself up and soon strangled.

The Gospels say that Jesus hung on the cross from noon until 3 PM, when he died. The Romans soldier confirmed his death by stabbing him in the side with a spear. They did not bother to break his legs, since he was already dead. At the moment of his death, the Gospels say, a powerful storm began, and the curtain that hid the holiest place in the Jewish temple was torn in two.

The Jewish authorities insisted that Jesus's body had to be taken down before the sun set, as the next day was the sabbath, a Jewish holy day on which no work could be done. Jesus's body was was taken down, wrapped in a sheet, and quickly placed in a tomb cut out of rock owned by a member of the Sanhedrin. A heavy stone was rolled

Eleventh century Italian painting of the disciples placing Jesus's body in the tomb.

over the opening. After the sabbath was over, Jesus's body would have to be properly prepared for burial and moved to its own tomb by his family and friends. Roman soldiers were ordered to guard the tomb to prevent anyone from entering the tomb.

The Resurrection

According to the Gospels, early on the day after the Jewish sabbath—Sunday—two women who were disciples of Jesus went to the tomb. They brought oils and spices used to pre-pare the body for burial. When they arrived they found the Roman soldiers sleeping. The heavy stone in front of the opening had been moved, and Jesus's body was gone.

The women hurried back to the city and told the disci-ples what they had seen. At first the apostles did not believe them. Peter and John rushed to the grave to verify what the women had told them. They too found the empty tomb, and returned to tell the other disciples. Soon, the Gospels relate, Jesus himself appeared to the disciples, to tell them he had risen from the dead.

Jesus spent the next forty days teaching the apostles and disciples. They came to understand that God had sent Jesus as the ultimate sacrifice, to redeem the sins of humanity.

Years earlier, on first seeing Jesus at the start of his pub-lic *ministry*, John the Baptist had proclaimed, "Look, the Lamb of God, who takes away the sins of the world!" This was a reference to a Jewish temple ritual in which an unblemished lamb was sacri-ficed to atone for sins. The meaning of John's statement was that Jesus—a person who had lived a sinless, perfect life—would atone for the sins of all humanity through his sac-rifice on the cross. Anyone who accepted Jesus and his teach-ings would have his or her sins forgiven and could develop a

Educational Video

To under-stand why Jesus is called the "Lamb of God," scan here:

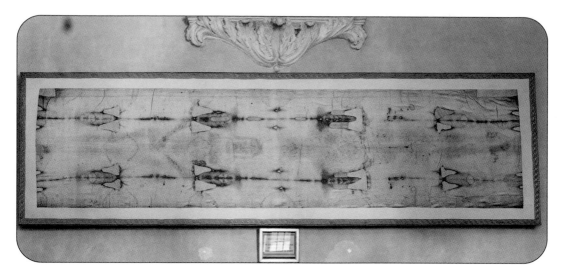

The Shroud of Turin is a 14-foot long piece of linen cloth that is viewed as a religious relic. Some Christians believe it was the burial cloth of Jesus, as it contains bloody marks that appear to be consistent with the wounds described in the New Testament, as well as faint images of a face and body. In 1898, when a photographer was allowed to take a picture of the shroud he noticed that details of the face were clearer on his photographic negative (opposite). However, scientific attempts to prove the Shroud's authenticity have been mixed, with some studies indicating it may have been a Medieval-era forgery.

closer relationship with God. Jesus explains this in a famous passage from the Gospel of John:

> For God so loved the world that he gave his one and only Son, that whoever believes in him shall not perish but have eternal life. For God did not send his Son into the world to condemn the world, but to save the world through him. Whoever believes in him is not condemned, but whoever does not believe stands condemned already because he has not believed in the name of God's one and only Son. This is the verdict: Light has come into the world, but men loved the darkness instead of light because their deeds were evil. Everyone who does evil hates the light, and will not come into the light for fear that his deeds will be exposed. But whoever lives by the truth comes into the light, so that it may be seen plainly that what he has done has been done through God. (John 3: 16–21)

At the end of the forty-day period of teaching, Jesus told his disciples to spread this message to all people. He promised them the assistance of the Holy Spirit, which God would send to inspire their ministry. Jesus then *ascended* into heaven, and his apostles went out to spread the message of salvation.

 Text-Dependent Questions

1. What are some of the signs that were observed at the birth of Jesus?
2. Where did Jesus live and teach?
3. What is Holy Week?

 Research Project

Using your school library or the internet, research the question, "Can someone really rise from the dead?" Those who believe this is possible may note that the people of Jesus's time would have laughed at such a claim if there was not a basis for truth to the Gospels. They might also say that some people have "died" during operations, but were later revived, showing that is is possible. Those who disagree may argue that there is no evidence for the resurrection, or that there are logical explanations for why Jesus's body was not in the tomb. Present your conclusion in a two-page report, providing examples from your research that support your answer.

 Words to Understand in This Chapter

creed—a formal statement of Christian belief.

epistle—a letter.

Gentiles—the name given to non-Jews by the Jews.

Pope—the bishop of Rome; the leader of the Roman Catholic Church.

Trinity—the presence of Three Persons (Father, Son and Holy Spirit) in one God.

The interior of Roman Catholic churches are often decorated with statues or artworks that depict religious scenes or important saints, such as this statue of the Apostle John and angels in the Duomo cathedral in Milan, Italy. Eastern Orthodox churches also have ornate statues, as well as religious paintings called icons. The interiors of Protestant churches tend to be much more simply decorated.

3 Development of the Christian Church

The original followers of Jesus were Jews who had heard him teach. Soon, *Gentiles* came to "The Way," as Christianity was called in its early days. They had heard about The Way from Jesus's followers and wanted to be baptized. People who accepted Jesus as their savior came to be known as Christians, a name derived from the Greek word for Messiah, *Christos*.

Jesus's original disciples believed that, after the crucifixion, the end of the world would soon come. When this did not happen right away, they began to write down Jesus's teachings so that later generations could learn them.

The sacred writings of Christianity are known as the Bible. The Christian Bible consists of two parts, which are called the Old Testament and the New Testament. The word *testament* means "promise," and Christians believe that God's promises to human beings are contained within the books of the Bible.

The Old Testament includes scriptures that are also sacred to Jews, such as the writings of Moses that include the Jewish law. The Old Testament also includes books written by the prophets who predicted the coming of the Messiah, as well as stories about David and the kings of Israel, and a collection of ancient songs praising God known as the psalms.

The New Testament includes the four Gospels—books about the life of Jesus, which were written by his disciples between thirty and sixty years after his death. Each of the gospels is named for its author: Matthew, Mark, Luke, or John. The Gospels include the teachings of Jesus and the beliefs of the original disciples. The New Testament also includes several other books. One book, the Acts of the Apostles, gives an account of the disciples just after the death of Jesus. Another, the Revelation of John, looks towards the end of time, predicting the return of Jesus and establishment of his kingdom. The New Testament also includes twenty-one *epistles*, or letters, to Christians written by early teachers such as Paul, James, and Jude, as well as by the apostles Peter and John.

Among the letter-writers, Paul is the most prolific. Thirteen of the twenty-one epistles in the New Testament are attributed to Paul, although modern scholars believe that some of the letters were actually written by Paul's disciples. Paul was an educated Jew who converted to

Gospels for Different Audiences

The Gospels—the four books in the Christian New Testament that detail the life and ministry of Jesus—were written several decades after Jesus's death. Each of the Gospels is written for a different audience.

A Christian missionary named Mark wrote the earliest gospel, the Gospel of Mark. This book, which focuses on the miracles and actions of Jesus's life, is written for a non-Jewish audience. Mark was not an apostle, but scholars believe that he worked in Rome with the Apostle Peter, who may have provided firsthand details of Jesus's life.

The Gospel of Matthew is written to for a Jewish audience. It is attributed to Matthew, a Jewish tax collector who was one of the Twelve Apostles. Matthew uses many references from the Jewish scriptures to show his readers that Jesus is the Messiah.

The author of the longest gospel, Luke, was an educated Greek doctor who served as a missionary in modern-day Greece and Turkey. Luke also wrote the Acts of the Apostles, a New Testament book that provides an account of the early Christian Church.

The gospels of Matthew, Mark, and Luke are called the "synoptic gospels," because they all contain many of the same stories and sayings of Jesus. Scholars think the authors may have referred to a list of Jesus's sayings when they wrote these gospels. The Gospel of John is attributed to another of the original Twelve Apostles. It contains more of Jesus's actual words than the other gospels. It also includes some stories that are not found in the other gospels.

Christianity after the death of Jesus, and became one of the most important leaders of the early church.

Growth of the Early Church

According to Acts of the Apostles, after Jesus's ascension the apostles returned to Jerusalem. They were together in one place when the Holy Spirit descended upon them. Under the leadership of Peter, to whom Jesus had given a leading place among the apostles, they began to speak to others about Jesus Christ. First they spoke in the Jerusalem Temple, preaching to the Jews and performing miracles through the power of the Holy Spirit.

Jewish leaders were not happy that Jesus's followers had maintained their beliefs, which they considered to be blasphemous and heretical. The Sanhedrin ordered that the apostles be arrested, but Acts records that they were miraculously freed from prison. In one case, however, a Christian named Stephen was placed on trial before the Sanhedrin. When Stephen stated that Jesus was the Son of God, the angry Jews took him outside the Temple and murdered him.

Acts of the Apostles says that this event set off a great wave of persecution against Christians, forcing many to flee from Jerusalem. A leader of this persecution was a devout Pharisee named Saul of Tarsus, who had been involved in the murder of Stephen. But while Saul was on the way to Damascus to attack the Christians there, he was struck blind. Then Saul heard Jesus speaking to him. Jesus told him to stop persecuting his followers.

Saul was stunned. According to letters that he later wrote to Christian churches, he spent several years reading the Jewish scriptures, and came to believe that Jesus was the Messiah and the fulfillment of prophecy. During this time, Jesus even appeared to him personally to teach him The Way.

With his sight recovered and now known by the name Paul, he became one of the most important teachers and missionaries of early Christianity. Between 46 and 64 CE

The Early Christian Church

Entry into The Way was by baptism. Jesus had been baptized at the beginning of his ministry and Christians wanted to be "washed clean" of their past life. New Christians would say they believed Jesus was Lord, that there was One God, Father, Son and Holy Spirit, and that Jesus had risen from the dead.

Paul wrote in one of his letters: "If there is no resurrection, then Christ was not raised; and if Christ was not raised, then our Gospel is null and void, as is your faith." So to state a belief that Jesus rose from the dead was—and remains—a vital commitment for Christians. This belief would be revealed in the way that Christians would treat each other. They believed that as God had shown his love by sending his son, Jesus, to Earth, they should show their love for God by loving each other. According to the Acts of the Apostles, members of the early Church shared all their possessions, food, and life together.

The Risen Christ is flanked by the apostles Peter (left) and Paul. Peter is depicted holding keys, symbolically representing that Jesus gave him the "keys to the kingdom" by making him the leader of the Twelve Apostles. Paul is represented holding a book, because of his many writings in the New Testament, as well as a sword, representing his martyrdom. Tradition holds that Paul was beheaded in Rome around the year 68 CE.

Paul traveled throughout the Roman world to spread the faith and establish churches. He wrote letters to the leaders of these churches, in which he set out the doctrine that would form the basis of Christianity.

Before Paul began his mission to the Gentiles, it was possible that Jesus's followers might eventually return to the greater Jewish community. They continued to worship God in the Temple and obeyed the Jewish law and scriptures along with Jesus's teachings.

Paul did a great deal to change this. He had been born a Jew, but he was also a Roman citizen and an admirer of Hellenistic culture. In his letters Paul explained that Jesus had come to replace Jewish law as the way to God. Salvation, he taught, came through faith in Jesus rather than in obedience to the law. All people, not just the Jews, could therefore be freed from their sin, and it became Paul's mission to spread this "good news" to the Gentile world. Paul wrote that the Jewish law had become a curse, for no man could fulfill its 613 commands and prohibitions completely. Therefore, it made sinners of everyone.

Paul taught that anyone—regardless of racial or cultural background, gender, or social position—who accepted Jesus would in turn be chosen by God. This was a significant break from Judaism, which taught that Jews were God's people and had been chosen for greatness as long as they kept the law. Mainstream Judaism also could not accept the idea of Jesus as divine—this was inherently offensive to a religion based on the belief in one God. Most Jews did not convert, and eventually they excluded the Christians from their synagogues. The Christians then had to find their own places to meet and worship.

The rate of conversion was much greater among the Gentiles. Many of the Roman Empire's Greek-speaking people had been attracted to the monotheism and ethical code of Judaism, but had never accepted all of its rituals and dietary laws. Christianity

Educational Video

To see how Christianity spread around the world, scan here

offered an attractive alternative, and soon Christian communities were established in many cities throughout the empire.

The spread of Christianity attracted the attention of Rome. Roman authorities saw Christianity as a threat to their control. The emperors believed in dealing quickly and efficiently with any movement that might cause political unrest. Christianity posed a potential threat because the movement was not confined to Judea. Imperial leaders construed Christians' refusal to follow the Roman custom and worship the emperors as gods as a sign that the Christians were disloyal to the empire and might be planning to revolt. Christianity's simple message of repentance and charity was also antithetical to the lavish and dissolute lifestyles of many Romans.

Persecution by Roman Authorities

For nearly 300 years, Christians were often persecuted by the Roman authorities. They chose secret signs to recognize each other, such as the fish. The letters of the Greek word for fish, *ichthys*, represented an anagram for "Jesus Christ, Son of God, Savior." Other early Christian signs included a boat or an anchor.

As Christianity grew, an organization began to develop. Small groups of Christians met secretly in the homes of believers, where they shared a meal and worshiped. These became the first churches. Within each church, certain members were given positions of responsibility. Presbyters, or priests, were appointed to be in charge of a church con-

Peter, First Among the Apostles

One of the first of the Twelve Apostles called by Jesus was a fisherman named Simon. The Gospel of Matthew relates how this apostle was the first to acknowledge Jesus as the promised Messiah. From that point, Jesus called him as Peter, from the Greek word *petros* ("rock"), saying that it was on the solid rock of faith that the Christian church would be built.

Clearly, Peter was a leader of the apostles. Every time the Twelve Apostles are listed by name in the New Testament, Peter is always first. He is at times referred to as the apostles' spokesman. In addition, Jesus often took Peter and two other apostles, James and John, along to experience events that the other apostles were not included in. These three apostles were with Jesus the night he was arrested in the Garden of Gethsemane, for example.

Peter was not perfect. Jesus rebuked him at times. After Jesus's arrest, when some men accused Peter of being one of his followers, he denied three times that he even knew Jesus. But after the Resurrection, Jesus forgave Peter.

Peter was one of the main leaders of the early church. The Apostle Paul wrote that Peter had the special charge of being apostle to the Jews, just as Paul was apostle to the Gentiles. Christian tradition holds that Peter founded a church in Antioch (present-day Syria), then traveled to Rome where he and Paul together established a Christian church there. Peter is considered the first bishop of Rome. Tradition holds that he was martyred there around the year 64 CE.

This stained glass window in the Saint Gatien Cathedral of Tours, France, depicts Christians being martyred by soldiers.

gregation. Deacons were selected in each church to carry out charitable works. A bishop was appointed to each city or region to oversee what was being taught in the churches there. These roles would be developed much more in the following centuries.

Persecution of Christians was more intense during certain periods. During the rule of the Roman emperor Nero (54–68 CE), Peter, Paul, and many of the apostles were executed. In 91 the emperor Domitian ordered attacks on Christians within the empire. During the rule of Marcus Aurelius, Christianity was made illegal in order to appease Rome's ancient gods after a rebellion by the Parthians. Other particularly severe persecutions of Christians occurred around 257 under Valerian, and from 303 to 313 under Diocletian.

The fact that Christians were so dedicated to their belief in Jesus that they were willing to die for the faith made others curious, however. Many people converted when they learned more about Christianity. "The blood of the martyrs is the seed of the church," wrote a Roman named Tertullian, who became a Christian in 197. But early in the fourth century Christianity's standing in Roman society would change dramatically, thanks to the influence of a powerful benefactor.

Constantine Legalizes Christianity

When Diocletian became emperor of Rome in 284, the empire was facing serious military and economic troubles. He instituted a program of reforms that included separating the empire into eastern and western divisions. Diocletian took control of the eastern half of the empire and installed an associate to rule in the West. Eventually, he created positions for two lesser leaders (caesars) who served under the eastern and western emperors. This established a form of

Statue of Constantine the Great, the Roman emperor who legitimized the Christian Church. Constantine's support enabled the religion to expand, and helped Christianity to eventually become the official religion of the Roman Empire.

government called the Tetrarchy, in which four rulers (the two eastern and two western tetrarchs) had a great deal of power.

After Diocletian's rule ended in 305, a power struggle broke out among the empire's rulers. After a long struggle Constantine—the son of one of the western tetrarchs—eventually emerged as the sole ruler of the Roman Empire. Constantine attributed his success to divine intervention. Before an important battle in 312, Constantine saw a sign in the sky that he believed was sent by Jesus Christ, and he told his soldiers to place the symbol XP (the Greek letters Chi and Rho, the first two letters of Christos) on their shields. Winning the battle helped Constantine capture Rome and gave him control over the western half of the empire.

With gratitude Constantine, joined by the eastern tetrarch Licinius, in 313 issued the Edict of Milan, which declared that the Roman Empire would not discriminate against any religion and would cease persecution of Christians. This gave the religion greater legitimacy and led to explosive growth in the Christian population.

The struggle for control over the empire was not over, however. It was not until 324 that Constantine defeated his rival Licinius and became the sole ruler. Constantine soon set to work establishing an eastern capital, which was built on the site of an ancient Greek city called Byzantium. The city, renamed Constantinople, was closer than Rome to the most heavily populated parts of the empire, and in 330 it became the imperial capital.

The Council of Nicaea

Although Constantine did not immediately become a Christian, he remained interested in the religion. He was upset when he learned that Christian leaders disagreed on many theological questions. In 325 he invited several hundred of the major Christian leaders to a council at which the core beliefs of Christianity would be established once and for all.

Christian thinkers had begun to disagree over theological matters early in church history. There had been numerous variant movements within Christianity. One of the more famous of these was Gnosticism, a belief system influenced by Greek and Eastern thought in which the intellect was considered divine and the physical world evil. Gnostics rejected many of the basic Christian teachings and were therefore condemned by mainstream Christian leaders.

The nature of Jesus was another question faced by early theologians. How could Christians reconcile worshipping Jesus as the divine Son of God when Jesus himself taught that humans should worship only one God? Was Jesus a man who became God through his suffering, or had he always been God? To explain this mystery, early church leaders developed the doctrine of the *Trinity*. This explained that the world and all things in it had been created by a single all-powerful God, but that He was composed of three parts: the Father, the Son, and the Holy Spirit. Each element of the Trinity was fully God, and therefore equally knowledgeable and powerful.

The doctrine of the Trinity was difficult for both Christians and non-Christians to understand. Some people believed that the Son and the Holy Spirit were less powerful than the Father because they had been created by God and did His bidding. In the early fourth century a Christian priest from Alexandria named Arius began to teach that Jesus, though divine, was a separate entity subservient to God. This teaching, called Arianism, was accepted by some church leaders and rejected by others.

The dispute threatened to split the church, so Constantine encouraged Christian bishops to gather at Nicaea, a lakeside village in modern-day Turkey. At the Council of Nicaea, the church leaders rejected Arianism and adopted a *creed* that stated the basic beliefs of Christianity. With only minor modifications, this creed remains the basic Christian belief today.

There were other issues that divided Christianity. Churches in the eastern part of the empire observed rites and festivals that differed from the rites and festivals observed by churches in the western part, for example. The Council of Nicaea addressed these practices with the intention of standardizing them throughout the entire church.

Rosaries, most often used nowadays by Roman Catholics to focus their thoughts on God when they are praying, were originally used by Eastern Christian monks in the third century CE. Similar kinds of prayer beads are used by Buddhists, Hindus, and Muslims.

The Nicene Creed

The Nicene Creed is a statement of Christian belief, adopted by the bishops at the Council of Nicaea in 325 and modified at the Council of Constantinople in 381. It clearly sets out Christian doctrine to distinguish it from heresy. The Creed is as follows:

We believe in one God, the Father, the Almighty, maker of heaven and earth, of all that is, seen and unseen.

We believe in one Lord, Jesus Christ, the only Son of God, eternally begotten of the Father, God from God, Light from Light, true God from true God, begotten, not made, one in Being with the Father.

Through Him all things were made. For us men and for our salvation He came down from heaven: by the power of the Holy Spirit He was born of the Virgin Mary, and became man.

For our sake He was crucified under Pontius Pilate; He suffered, died, and was buried. On the third day He rose again in fulfillment of the Scriptures; He ascended into heaven and is seated at the right hand of the Father. He will come again in glory to judge the living and the dead, and His kingdom will have no end.

We believe in the Holy Spirit, the Lord, the giver of life, who proceeds from the Father and the Son. With the Father and the Son He is worshiped and glorified. He has spoken through the Prophets.

We believe in one holy catholic and apostolic Church. We acknowledge one baptism for the forgiveness of sins. We look for the resurrection of the dead, and the life of the world to come. Amen.

When the council ended, Constantine thanked Christian leaders for agreeing on dogma. However, this did not end disputes over theological matters. Arianism, for example, spread to the Germanic tribes outside the empire, where it persisted as a variant Christian belief.

Constantine helped Christianity in many ways. He exempted the church from certain taxes and contributed to the construction of ornate basilicas in Rome, Jerusalem, and other places throughout the empire. He eventually outlawed pagan sacrifices and the worship of idols. His patronage encouraged many Romans to convert, as Constantine himself did just before he died in 337.

But there was a downside to Constantine's influence on the church. His role in calling the Council of Nicaea and his interest in resolving other church disputes set a precedent for government involvement in religion. And his support for Christianity led many politically minded people to join the religion to further their career ambitions, rather than because they believed in its teachings.

Within the empire, Christianity gradually became the religion of choice for most people. It spread outside the empire as well, and by the middle of the fourth century it had been embraced by many of the Germanic tribes living on the fringes of Roman power.

Empire and Church Divided

Although Constantine had reunited the empire under his rule, after 395 the empire became permanently divided into eastern and western halves. There were many social differences between the two parts of the empire. Even the languages were different: Latin was spoken in Rome and the West, while Greek was the language of Constantinople and the East. But during the fourth and fifth centuries both sections of the empire were under growing pressure from outside forces. The "barbarian" Goths and Franks attacked the frontiers of the western empire, while to the east the empire had to deal with the growing strength of the Sassanid Persians. There were internal problems as well: regular civil wars over control of the empire and high taxes to support the large military. These factors kept the Roman Empire in a near-constant state of unrest.

Christianity officially became the state religion in 381, and other religions were outlawed. However, because in ancient Rome the rulers had also been pontifex maximus, or leader of the state religion, the emperors felt entitled to involve themselves in religious matters.

Over centuries, Christianity developed a sophisticated organization of church leaders. In the original churches established by the apostles, local leaders had been chosen to teach the believers, lead worship services, and induct new members into their community. By the third century, however, a hierarchy of church leaders was established to govern the Christian community more efficiently. A priest was appointed to lead each individual church. A bishop would oversee the activities of all of the churches in a particular city or region, to make sure priests were following the accepted church teachings. The bishops of Alexandria, Antioch, Jerusalem, Constantinople, and Rome were con-

Pope Francis waves to a crowd of the faithful in St. Peter's Square, Vatican City. As bishop of Rome, the pope is the the spiritual successor to the Apostle Peter and leader of the Roman Catholic Church.

sidered the most important, because they led the largest Christian communities or apostles had founded their churches. The accepted practice was for smaller communities faced with doctrinal questions they could not resolve to appeal to the closest major bishopric for a ruling on the issue.

The Roman church had a connection to two apostles: Peter and Paul had both been executed in Rome during Nero's rule. In the third century a church leader named

The Orthodox Church is the second-largest Christian denomination, with approximately 270 members in total. It is divided into a number of regional churches, such as the Russian (150 million), Romanian (23 million), or Greek (15 million) churches. Four cities important in early Christianity—Alexandria (Egypt), Constantinople (Turkey), Jerusalem (Israel), and Antioch (Syria) also have their own self-governing church communities. The Orthodox Church does not have a single leader; instead, each of the regional churches is led by a head bishop (often called a patriarch) and a council of bishops (called a Holy Synod). The patriarch of Constantinople is considered one of the most important Orthodox leaders; Bartholomew I, pictured above, is the 270th bishop to hold that office.

Irenaeus claimed that Peter had been the first bishop of Rome, and that because of Peter's importance in the early church the Roman bishop (who eventually became known as the *Pope*) should be considered the final authority for all decisions related to church doctrine. Because Rome was the most important bishopric in the western empire, its leadership was ultimately accepted by the churches of western Europe and North Africa.

The eastern Christian churches did not accept Rome's supremacy, however. They preferred to resolve disagreements over doctrine through consensus of church leaders. To achieve consensus, they called ecumenical councils of bishops. These first of these was the Council of Nicaea in 325; other important early councils were held at Constantinople (381), Ephesus (431), and Chalcedon (451). Although representatives of the Roman church participated at these councils, in which orthodox doctrine was established, they had no more influence than any other bishops.

By the fifth century the Byzantine Empire, as the eastern part of the empire came to be called, was the uncontested center of imperial power. The wealthiest provinces, such as Syria and Egypt, were located in the east, and the tax revenue they provided allowed Byzantine emperors to equip armies and protect their territories. The western emperors had fewer resources and so could not prevent invasions by Germanic tribes. Rome itself had fallen into decline, and the capital of the western empire was moved to Milan. As the western empire grew weaker, the popes gained greater power over both religious and secular life. When the Huns threatened Rome in 452, for example, it was Pope Leo, rather than the western emperor, who convinced their leader Attila not to attack the city. But even the church could not stop the ultimate collapse of the western empire in 476, when the last Roman emperor was deposed by invading German tribes.

The "fall" of the empire did not immediately cause an upheaval in European life. Rome itself was hardly damaged, and the lives of most people continued relatively unchanged. Many of the Germanic peoples had respected Roman laws and culture. Most tribal leaders had accepted Christianity—although of the variant form of Arianism—and they expected Christian bishops and priests to maintain order in their cities.

Divisions in the Church

Despite the collapse of the western empire, in the east Constantinople remained at the center of a brilliant civilization. The Byzantine Empire would survive the fall of Rome by nearly 1,000 years. But as differences in doctrine emerged, the two major branches of Christianity grew further apart. Although the eastern and western churches would remain in contact over the next 600 years, by 1054 Christianity officially separated into two churches: the Roman Catholic and Eastern Orthodox, each of which believed its was the "true" church based on apostolic tradition and teachings.

Christianity would undergo other divisions in the centuries that followed. The most significant break occurred during the 16th century, when there arose a great 'protest' about abuses in the Roman Catholic Church. People such as Martin Luther, a Roman Catholic monk from Germany, and the Frenchman John Calvin led opposition to certain practices of the Roman Catholic leadership. It was a time of upheaval in Europe. The invention of the printing press made the Bible more available and there was social unrest. The time was ripe for a change. The reform movement

The churches of Protestant Christian denominations are often built in a simpler style than Roman Catholic or Orthodox churches. Many feature red doors. Major Protestant denominations include Baptists, Lutherans, Methodists, and Presbyterians. In total, the number of Protestant Christians in the various churches is about 800 million.

Martin Luther was a German priest, who objected to what he considered corrupt practices in the Roman Catholic Church. In 1517 he nailed a list of his religious objections to the door of the church in Wittenberg. People who agreed with Luther established new Christian churches that did not accept the Roman pope's authority. Today, most members of the Lutheran Church live in Scandinavia, Germany, or the United States.

became known as the Protestant Reformation.

Over the next two centuries, such Protestant denominations as the Lutherans, Presbyterians, and Baptists were established, as well as the Religious Society of Friends (also known as Quakers), and the Methodists.

During the 1530s, the Church of England (the Anglican Church) broke from the Church in Rome over the unwillingness of the Pope to accept the divorce of the English king, Henry VIII. As this Church took shape, it retained many Catholic practices in worship but adopted some Protestant attitudes, too, including a desire to be free from the control of the Roman Catholic pope. For this reason, the Church of England is often regarded as a bridge between the Roman and Protestant Churches. In the United States, the Anglican Church is often called the Episcopal Church.

During the early twentieth century, the Pentecostal movement emerged in African-American communities. Pentecostals believe the Holy Spirit of God gives them power to heal and preach the Gospels. They are noted for their powerful singing and emotional services.

The beliefs of all Christian churches are very similar. Christians believe in the divinity and resurrection of Jesus Christ, and accept the basic creeds of Christianity that were established at the Council of Nicaea and other councils many years ago. The differences between churches are mainly those of worship and of the authority of the Church, and many reflect the culture and environment of the followers. So the differences are mainly of interpretation and what has grown up around the Churches over the centuries. It is rather like a family in which there will be much agreement and acceptance of differences with the occasional argument that needs to be settled with tact and sympathy.

 Text-Dependent Questions

1. In what year did Christianity become the official religion of the Roman Empire?
2. What was the Protestant Reformation?

 Research Project

Using the Internet or your school library, research the life of an important figure from the early days of Christianity, such as Peter, Paul, John, James, Barnabas, Clement, or one of the other apostles. Write a two-page report about this person and present it to your class.

 ## Words to Understand in This Chapter

absolution—God's forgiveness after a Confession.

confession—the formal admission of one's wrongdoings or sins, often to a priest.

Confirmation—the act of confirming the promises to follow the Christian faith that were made at one's baptism.

Eucharist—the central act of Christian worship, the sharing of bread and wine to share in the life of the risen Jesus Christ. Also known as Holy Communion, the Lord's Supper, or the Mass.

Holy Week—the seven days leading up to Easter Sunday.

Lent—the period of 40 days (not including Sundays) of fasting and repentance leading up to Easter.

sacrament—a sign of the presence of Jesus Christ. The Roman Catholic and Orthodox churches consider the seven sacraments to be Baptism, Confirmation, Holy Communion, Confession, Marriage, Ordination, and Healing. Protestant churches tend to accept just Baptism and Communion as sacraments.

sermon—a religious talk.

4 Services and Sacraments

Christians celebrate their faith by going to church, reading the Bible, and observing festivals and fasts that commemorate the main events of the Christian year. They also express their beliefs by bringing up their children in the faith and marrying in church. Some Christians are ordained as priests or ministers.

All Christians want to mark important times in their life by re-affirming and re-dedicating their lives to God. The important moments surround birth, entry into adulthood, marriage, and death. They are called "rites of passage" because they mark the transition when a person moves from one stage to another.

Some Christians attend church services every day. Others go once a week, although they may go to church more often during special times in the Church's year.

Christians have their main worship on Sunday because that was the day Jesus rose from the dead.

Worship Services

Liturgy, or public worship services, are regular events during which Christians sing, listen to teachings, say prayers, confess their wrongdoings to God, and give God thanks for the good things in life.

Roman Catholics call the worship service the Mass. Some Orthodox churches, as well as a few Protestant denominations, also use this term. Eastern Orthodox churches call the worship service the Divine Liturgy. The Anglican and Episcopal churches call its services the *Eucharist*, from the Greek for "thanksgiving." Many Protestant or Pentecostal churches simply call this event a church service or a worship service.

Most services follow a set order of events. Services often begin with the singing of hymns or praise songs, followed by prayers for the community and one or more readings from the Bible. The order of services can vary from denomination to denomination, and even among churches within a particular denomination. Pentecostal churches tend to be more relaxed than other churches when it comes to the schedule of the service.

The Bible is read during most services. Usually there are readings from the Old and New Testaments, especially from the Gospels. In many churches, the congregation stands when the Gospel is read. Because Christians believe the Bible is God's word, it has to be treated with reverence

Readings from the Bible are an important part of Christian services.

and care. The congregants listen carefully to the readings and try to apply what they hear to their own lives. After the Gospel reading, the priest or minister delivers a *sermon*, or short discussion of the Gospel message.

In the Roman Catholic, Orthodox, and Anglican churches, the readings are followed by a ritual known as Holy Communion. On the altar in front of the congregation, the priest symbolically breaks bread and drinks wine, with the people participating in prayers. The bread and wine are then shared with all members of the church. This part of the service is a reminder of Jesus's Last Supper with his disciples, when he asked them to remember him whenever they ate bread and drank wine together. The bread is said to represent the broken body of Jesus Christ, while the wine represents his blood that was shed on the cross to save humanity.

The Roman Catholic Church and some Orthodox churches believe that in some mysterious way the bread and wine actually become Jesus's body and blood during the Communion ritual. This belief is called transubstantiation. Roman Catholic churches offer communion to the faithful at every Mass.

Protestant churches do not agree with the concept of transubstantiation, but they do hold a communion-type

These adults who have prepared to join an Eastern Orthodox church are being baptized in the Jordan River in Israel—the same river where Jesus was baptized.

meal of bread and wine at some services. In Protestant tradition, this is sometimes called "the Lord's Supper," and it is a very special memorial meal that Christians must observe to remember the sacrifice of Jesus. Some Protestant churches include this communion as part of every service; others do it less regularly—every month or every two months, for example.

Many churches also hold children's services and midweek meetings for prayer or social groups. For many Christians, churchgoing is for reflection, a time to think about their lives and their relationship with God. They may be in difficult times or have hard decisions to make and feel the need to talk to God about them. Church services, or the quiet peaceful atmosphere and the support of other Christians, can give people the time and space to do so.

The Sacraments

The dictionary defines a *sacrament* as an oath of allegiance, an obligation, or a formal religious act as a sign of belief. The Roman Catholic and Eastern Orthodox churches recognize seven sacraments—Baptism, Holy Communion, Confirmation, Marriage, Confession, Healing, and Ordination. Most Protestant denominations only recognize two sacraments—Baptism and the Lord's Supper, because Jesus took part in them during his lifetime.

Baptism

Baptism is the outward sign that a person has become a Christian. Virtually all Christians will be baptized at the start of their Christian journey. Putting water on the forehead or going down under the water and then rising up is done to symbolize the washing away of past wrongdoing and being reborn as a follower of Jesus Christ.

The first Christians were baptized as adults but, as time went by, parents wanted babies to be accepted as well. The older Churches—the Roman Catholic and Orthodox—baptize babies, as do the Anglican churches. Traditional churches use a font and pour water over the baby's head. The Orthodox Churches make sure that the baby is entirely immersed. By contrast, some of the Protestant Churches believe that a person cannot become a full member of the Church before they are old enough to make promises for themselves. So the Baptist Church, for example, baptizes adults in a baptistery—a pool laid in the floor of the church building.

In the early Church, Baptism had to take place in moving water to make visible the movement of the Holy Spirit in human life. This is why today, in warmer countries, Baptism often takes place outdoors in flowing rivers and streams.

Confession and First Communion

In the Roman Catholic Church, children around the age of eight take part in two important ceremonies. Once they complete a period of religious instruction, they are given the sacrament of *confession*. This is the opportunity to tell their sins to a priest (their confessor), who listens in confidence on God's behalf. Penitents must speak honestly and be truly sorry if they are to be given *absolution*. When they are done, penitents are given a penance by the confessor, which is often the saying of specified prayers, to atone for their wrongdoings.

Confession of sins is an important prerequisite for another major event in a Roman Catholic child's life. After some additional religious education, the child goes through a First Holy Communion ceremony. This is the first time the child is permitted to share the bread and wine at a church service. Children dress in fine clothes for the ceremony—girls in white dresses, boys in white shirts, ties, and dark trousers.

Young girls participate in the First Holy Communion service in a Roman Catholic church.

A Christian may not share in communion in a Roman Catholic church unless he or she has completed a First Holy Communion ceremony. Thus, a Protestant visitor to a Catholic church cannot share in the bread and wine. Catholics are also expected to confess their sins before taking communion. Many do so on Saturday afternoon so they are prepared to attend Mass on Sunday morning.

Confirmation

Confirmation is an event in which Christians confirm their religious beliefs. When a baby is baptized, the godparents and parents make promises to be a good Christian on behalf of the child. When the child is older, he or she will be able to confirm those vows for themselves. The person being confirmed will have taken some instruction in the faith to make sure they are fully aware of their commitment and that they are doing it with free will. Confirmation usually takes place in front of a bishop, who places his or her hands on the person's head, blesses them and receives them into full membership of the Church. Confirmation can take place from the age of about 10 onwards.

Marriage

The details of Christian wedding ceremonies can vary, depending on the church. For all Christian couples, the most important aspect of the ceremony is that the bride and bridegroom make promises to each other before God. The wedding is considered to be the unification of two people, body and soul, in the presence of friends and relatives and before God. The couple exchange promises of faithfulness, and to love and support each other whatever the future brings. Marriage is for mutual support and the upbringing of children, and prayers are offered on behalf of the couple.

Educational Video

Scan to hear a Roman Catholic priest explain Holy Communion:

Roman Catholic teaching states: "The intimate union of marriage . . . demands total fidelity from the spouses and requires an unbreakable unity between them." Divorce is not recognized by the Roman Catholic Church except in extreme circumstances. However, other churches have a more relaxed view of divorce and will, under certain conditions, allow divorced people to be re-married in the church.

Ordination and Healing

Ordination refers to the appointment of a person as a preacher or authority in the church. Some people believe they are called by God to be priests or ministers. If the Church considers a person suitable, they begin training before being ordained in a special ceremony. The new minister will then work under someone with more experience for a time.

The sacrament of healing is also known as "anointing of the sick." It involves placing a small amount of a special oil that has been blessed by a Roman Catholic priest on the forehead of a person who is suffering a severe illness. The priest also recites certain prayers, asking for God's healing and grace.

Although Protestants do not consider this a sacrament, in many Protestant churches the practice of "laying on of hands" is common. A person who is suffering from a severe illness may come to the front of the church, either during or after a worship service. The deacons and elders of the church, along with the minister, will put their hands on the person and pray together for him or her to be healed, if that is God's will.

The Last Rites is a ritual in the Roman Catholic church for a person who is near death. The priest anoints the sick person, and says prayers asking God to forgive the dying person's sins, so that he or she is ready to enter the presence of God after death. The sign of the cross is made on their forehead, mouth and chest.

The Christian View of Death

Christians believe that when Jesus comes again they will rise from the dead. This is why, traditionally, Christians are buried, not cremated. In fact, the Orthodox Churches do not allow cremation. Funerals can be very sad times, especially for those who have a relative or a close friend who has died. Some Christians, however, see funerals as a joyous occasion, for they are certain that the dead person has gone to heaven to live with God forever. They have not died; spiritually they have moved on to be with God and to begin a new and better life.

Most church funeral services include prayers and a short talk about the dead person before burial in the churchyard or cemetery. Gravestones in churchyards are usually put up several weeks after a burial to allow the ground to settle. There are rules and regulations about the design of the headstone and what can be written on it; these vary with each Church and individual priest or vicar.

Holidays and Festivals

The major holy days in the Christian calendar commemorate important events in the life of Jesus. All churches celebrate the two main festivals, Easter and Christmas. Others festivals, such as feast days dedicated to particular saints, and harvest festivals, are celebrated by some churches but not others.

The Easter season is a time in which Christians remember the events surrounding the crucifixion, death, and resurrection of Jesus. It comes after a time of preparation called *Lent*. According to the Gospels, Jesus spent 40 days fasting and praying in the desert before he started teaching. Lent is a 40-day period during which children and adults may give up sweets or other favorite treats as a symbolic sacrifice. They will also say prayers and read their Bibles more regularly.

The final week of Lent is known as *Holy Week*. It begins with Palm Sunday, which commemorates Jesus's arrival in Jerusalem. On Holy Thursday, also called Maundy Thursday, Christians remember the Last Supper. Jesus was crucified on Good Friday—it is called by this name because

In some predominantly Roman Catholic countries, Christians re-enact the events of Holy Week publicly. Here, an actor portraying Jesus carries the cross while being beaten by Roman soldiers in Gora Kalwaria, Poland.

because Jesus willingly sacrificed himself to save humanity. On Easter Sunday, the day Jesus rose from the dead, there are church services for families and there are special times at home: cards, good wishes and, for some, the excitement of getting up early to watch for the dawn on Easter Day with the joy of saying, "Christ is risen." The dates of the Easter season vary from year to year, because they are calculated according to a lunar calendar so that they align with the Jewish festival of Passover.

Unlike Easter, Christmas is always celebrated on the same date every year, December 25. Christmas marks the birth of Jesus. The four weeks before Christmas are called the season of Advent, and during this time churches often stage Nativity plays that depict the birth of Jesus, or hold carol services in which songs of praise are sung. At Christmas there are services in churches, and families come together to celebrate the holiday. Many Christians make an effort to ensure that homeless or poor people have a place to go where they can be fed and kept warm.

Text-Dependent Questions

1. What is Holy Communion, and what does it represent?
2. What is the sacrament of Confirmation?
3. How long does the season of Lent last?

Research Project

Using your school library or the internet, research the question, "Should the Bible be open to new interpretation?" Some Christians believe that holy books such as the Bible that come from a certain period in history should be reinterpreted to make more sense to modern readers. If these books are to be relevant to us, they argue, they need to address the problems of today. Others note that the Bible was inspired by God, and in many places records the actual words of God, so it cannot be changed or interpreted according to modern values. Instead, these people believe, Christians must make a greater effort to study what God asks of His people, and then put that into practice. Present your conclusion in a two-page report, providing examples from your research that support your answer.

Words to Understand in This Chapter

intelligent design—a creationist theory that is compatible with evolution, but posits that God is the original creator, or "designer," of all life.

sacred tradition—customs and practices associated with Christian teaching through the ages. Protestant Christians tend to reject sacred tradition as authoritative, preferring to use the Bible as the sole source of guidance.

tithing—the practice of giving 10 percent of one's income to the Church.

Anti-abortion protesters march at the Texas state capitol building in Austin. Many Christians are opposed to abortion, believing that the unborn fetus is a life created by God and that to abort the fetus is akin to murder.

5 Challenges of the Modern World

The world has changed a great deal in the 2,000 years since Jesus was teaching his disciples in the Galilee region. Throughout that time, Christians have had to apply the teachings of Jesus to situations that were unknown or not thought of centuries earlier. Christians can, and do, arrive at different conclusions or interpretations of Biblical teachings.

There are several sources of authority and guidance for most Christians. The first place that Christians look for guidance is the Bible, to see what direction the teachings of Jesus can give. Sometimes there is no direct answer, and Christians must reflect on and interpret the Biblical text in relation to their own situation. There is also the authority of the particular denomination that a Christian belongs to. Some denominations provide very clear and firm guidance on specific issues. Others allow greater responsibility for the Christian to speak with God in private prayer. Another authoritative guide is *sacred tradition*—the customs and practices associated with Christian teaching down the ages. These sources mean that while there may be differences in the advice given on specific subjects, the Christian will still find support and guidance.

Charity

One of the most important things Christians can do is care for others. They believe that God loved the world so much that he sacrificed his son, Jesus, on the cross for them. In turn, the Christian must be prepared to do the same: sacrificing his or her life for God. This means that many Christians are involved in charities. Some work for Christian charities while others help small local charities or work with neighbors who need help and support.

In 1950, a Roman Catholic nun called Mother Teresa started the Order of the Missionaries of Charity in Calcutta, India. The order's members were dedicated to serving the poorest of the poor—the destitute, abandoned and dying of all castes and religions. Mother Teresa was awarded the 1979 Nobel Peace Prize.

Christian groups like the Salvation Army are devoted to helping the poor and homeless. While they hope to convert people to the Christian faith, their main activity is to serve and tend those in greatest need, regardless of their religious beliefs. For example, Mother Teresa, a Roman Catholic nun who became famous for her work in the slums of Calcutta, founded the Roman Catholic Order of the Sisters of Charity to help the very poorest people in India—most of whom are not Christian, but Hindu.

Some Christians give one-tenth of their income to charity; this is called *tithing*. Others give their time and energy

Some of the money collected by Christian churches during the worship services is used to help others. Funds could spent to support missionaries working in foreign countries, or could be used to help local people that are in need.

to the needy. Charity is a way of living their faith. Some Christians prefer acting out their commitment to Jesus in this way rather than going to church regularly.

Forgiveness

Just as charity comes from the love of God, so Christians believe that if a person wants God to forgive his or her own wrongdoing, then he or she has to be ready to forgive those who do wrong to them. Jesus, Christians believe, had the power to forgive sins or wrongdoing against God. Even on the cross at his crucifixion he asked God to forgive those responsible for executing him because they did not understand what they were doing. Jesus's teaching says that forgiveness is important, but for God to forgive a person, that person must be willing to forgive as well.

Forgiveness is not easy, and when one does wrong it is important to be truly sorry for one's actions and thoughts. Christians believe that, if a person tries not to repeat a wrongdoing, God will forgive him or her. Peter asked Jesus how many times he should forgive someone—seven? Jesus replied "Seventy times seven," meaning that forgiveness should be limitless. As long as that person is genuinely sorry, God will then forgive them likewise.

Women as Clergy

Ordination is the process by which individuals are consecrated, that is, set apart as clergy to perform various religious rites and ceremonies. Historically, most churches have ordained men to serve as priests or ministers. However, over

Men pause to find the name of a loved one on the black granite wall of the Vietnam Veterans Memorial in Washington, D.C. Visiting memorials can help with the process of healing and forgiveness.

Reverend Amy Butler speaks at a rally in New York City. In 2014 she became the first woman to hold the position of Senior Minister at the famous Riverside Church, an interdenominational church located in Upper Manhattan.

the past century many of the Protestant Christian denominations have begun to ordain women to serve as ministers or in leadership roles. These include the Presbyterian, Baptist, Lutheran, and Anglican (Episcopal) churches in the United Sates. Some of these denominations allow women to serve in higher leadership positions, as bishops, while others do not.

To date there are no women priests in the Roman Catholic or Orthodox churches. These two organizations have resisted women priests, arguing that Jesus chose only male apostles.

The Protestant churches also allow ministers to be married, unlike the Catholic and Orthodox priests, who must take a vow of celibacy. The priestly vow is a tradition that dates back to a very early period in the church. However, in the earliest days not all priests were celibate. The Apostle Peter, first bishop of Rome, was married. However, this is a rule that is unlikely to change any time soon in the Roman Catholic and Orthodox churches.

Views on Homosexuality

Jesus never spoke about homosexuality, but same-sex relationships were strongly forbidden by the Old Testament laws. Consequently, most Christians today are generally not supportive of homosexual behavior, believing it to be against the natural order God created. However, recent research has indicated that same-sex attraction is not something that people choose; there is a genetic component to homosexuality, and thus people actually are born that way naturally.

Some Christians believe sexual activity should only take place in the sanctity of marriage. They consider any sort of premarital sex to be sinful, whether it is heterosexual or homosexual. While many are sympathetic to people who

Orthodox Christians participate in an ecumenical service with Muslims and Jews in Turkey. In recent years, Christian Churches have worked hard to establish an understanding and rapport with other faiths and to make a commitment to the conservation of the environment.

are homosexual, they believe these individuals should not have sexual relations. Rather, they believe these people should remain celibate and accept their situation as their "cross to bear." Other, more liberal Christians, feel this is an unreasonable request that forces people to deny an essential part of their humanity.

There is a vigorous and unfinished debate among Christians about attitudes to homosexuality and whether homosexuals may be ordained as clergy. Most churches, including the Roman Catholic Church and the Orthodox churches, do not permit the ordination of openly gay or lesbian priests. However, some Protestant denominations have become more tolerant of ordaining homosexual pastors or ministers, including the Episcopal Church in the United States since the 1980s, the Evangelical Lutheran Church in America since 2010, and the Presbyterian Church (USA) since 2012.

In 2003, the Episcopal Church of the United States ordained an openly gay priest, Gene Robinson, as bishop of the Diocese of New Hampshire. This move was highly controversial and resulted in a schism within the Episcopal Church.

Abortion and Contraception

One of the fundamental beliefs of the Christian faith is that God created the world and everything in it. God creates life and only God has the right to take it away. Christian teaching is opposed to abortion, although some churches do allow exceptions. The Roman Catholic Church opposes abortion in all cases. Most other Churches also reject abortion but accept there may be exceptional circumstances, such as when the health of the mother is at risk. It is also partly a question of when life is believed to have begun. If it begins at the moment of conception, then any abortion can be regarded as the taking of life, but some scientists and clergy define life as beginning sometime after conception.

The Roman Catholic Church believes in the sanctity of all life. It is up to God to decide whether sexual intercourse should result in a child being conceived. The couple may

A doctor explains to a patient some different kinds of contraception and how they are administered. Such practices would be seen as sinful by Roman Catholics.

not therefore use any artificial means to stop conception for that is to take on the power of God to make decisions. There are, of course, couples who do practice contraception. The Roman Catholic Church has been under pressure to agree to the use of condoms to reduce the risk of sexually transmitted diseases, such as AIDS.

Other churches have less decided attitudes on these topics, and while some Protestant groups may have similar views to the Catholic Church, most regard contraception as a private matter of conscience.

Creationism versus Evolution

The Bible teaches that God created the world out of a formless void. The stories of creation show God being the architect of creation but giving human beings responsibility and stewardship over that creation. Creation is inspired by God's power—His spirit—but the Bible also instructs humans to to care for the world and for all of God's creation.

Until relatively recently, most Christians accepted these stories at face value. But in 1859 a scientist named Charles Darwin introduced the world to his theory of evolution with his book *On the Origin of Species*. His theory that every living thing on earth evolved over time through a process that he called called "natural selection" is now regarded as fact by most scientists.

Some Christians have no trouble accepting both of these premises: that God created the world as described in the Bible, and that the process of evolution is the most likely way that modern animals and plants developed from earlier forms of life. They note that the important thing is to have a relationship with God through his Son, Jesus Christ, and to live in the way that Jesus instructed his followers. Leaders of the Roman Catholic Church, including Pope John Paul II, have said that evolution is a

Educational Video

For an explanation of "intelligent design" theory, scan here:

legitimate scientific theory that is compatible with Catholic beliefs, so long as the believer recognizes that evolution is directed by God and that the soul is God's divine creation. The Episcopal, Presbyterian, United Methodist, and Evangelical Lutheran churches have taken similar official positions on evolution.

Other Christians take the Bible stories literally, and thus reject evolution completely. They have fought to prevent it from being taught in public schools. Over the years there have been a number of important court cases that deal with the teaching of evolution versus its religious-based alternatives, such as creationism or *intelligent design*. These include the 1925 Scopes trial in Tennessee, or more recent federal court cases like *Webster v. New Lenox School District* (1990) or *Kitzmiller v. Dover* (2005). American courts have consistently held that creationism cannot be taught in public schools because it violates the U.S. Constitution's prohibition against establishing or favoring a state religion.

A memorial outside the Orlando nightclub where a man named Omar Mateen killed 49 people and wounded 53 others in a terrorist attack/hate crime in October 2016. Despite God's love, people's inhumanity to one another and the suffering it causes continues.

Why Doesn't God Prevent Suffering?

Many people who are not Christians question the idea of a loving God who cares for all the people that He has created. If God loves us so much, they ask, why is there suffering in the world? Why do people—even devout Christians—die from cancer, lose their jobs, or experience tragedies in their personal lives?

The answer that most Christians would give to this question is, "only God knows." Christians believe in a God who came to Earth as a man and experienced the painful events of everyday living, while also suffering extraordinary agony on the cross when he died. This means that

Christianity has a suffering savior at its heart. Jesus could have avoided his suffering, but he did not: instead, he told God that he would be obedient to God's will. Jesus therefore is an example to Christians that whatever happens, they need to maintain their faith in God.

Christians try to help those who suffer by undertaking charitable work; they have founded hospitals and schools as well as organizations to support the poor and destitute. Ill health and natural disasters, for example, are reminders of the impermanence of life and that only faith in God brings security and the hope of a better life with God after death.

 Text-Dependent Questions

1. Why do the Roman Catholic and Eastern Orthodox churches only appoint male priests?
2. How do many Christians view evolution?

 Research Project

Using your school library or the internet, research the question, "Should you give to charity?" One perspective is that the world is unfair—the three wealthiest people in the world have more money than the 48 poorest countries combined, and millions of children die each year from poverty-related illnesses. So those who have more than they need should help those who lack enough resources to meet even basic needs. On the other hand, people deserve the money they have earned and should be able to spend it as they wish. Some people feel that charity demeans people and makes them dependent on others. Present your conclusion in a two-page report, providing examples from your research that support your answer.

Religious Demographics

U.S. & Canada about 5.6 million people

Canada about 25 million people

U.S. about 225 million people

U.S. about 0.575 million

North and South America about 10 million people

Latin America about 543 million people

Europe about 2.1 million people

Europe about 0.5 million people

Europe about 50 million people

Europe about 550 million people

Israel about 5.6 million people

Africa about 518 million people

Africa about 475 million people

Asia about 1179 million people

Asia about 350 million people

Asia about 550 million people

India about 18 million people

Asia about 950 million people

Australia and Oceania about 24 million people

Australia and Oceania about 0.7 million people

Christians
about 2.2 billion people

Muslims
about 1.6 billion people

Sikh
about 23 million people

Hindus
about 1 billion people

Jews
about 14 million people

Buddhist
about 576 million people

Christian	Islam	No religion	Hindu	Buddhist	Sikhism	Judaism	Others
31.5%	22.3%	15.4%	14.0%	5.3%	0.3%	0.2%	11%

Hinduism

Founded
Developed gradually in prehistoric times

Number of followers
Around 1 billion

Holy Places
River Ganges, especially at Varanasi
(Benares). Several other places in India

Holy Books
Vedas, Upanishads,
Mahabharata, Rarnayana

Holy Symbol
Aum

Buddhism

Founded
535 BCE in Northern India

Number of followers
Around 576 million

Holy Places
Bodh Gaya, Sarnath, both in northern India

Holy Books
Tripitaka

Holy Symbol
Eight-spoked wheel

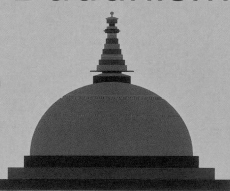

Sikhism

Founded
Northwest India, 15th century CE

Number of followers
Around 23 million

Holy Places
There are five important, takhts, or seats of
high authority: in Amritsar, Patna Sahib,
Anandpur Sahib, Nanded, and Talwandi

Holy Books
The Guru Granth Sahib

Holy Symbol
The Khanda, the symbol
of the Khalsa

Christianity

Founded
Around 30 CE, Jerusalem

Number of followers
Around 2.2 billion

Holy Places
Jerusalem and other sites
associated with the life of Jesus

Holy Books
The Bible
(Old and New Testament)

Holy Symbol
Cross

Judaism

Founded
In what is now Israel, around 2,000 BCE

Number of followers
Around 14 million

Holy Places
Jerusalem, especially
the Western Wall

Holy Books
The Torah

Holy Symbol
Seven-branched menorah (candle stand)

Islam

Founded
610 CE on the Arabian Peninsula

Number of followers
Around 1.6 billion

Holy Places
Makkah and Madinah, in Saudi Arabia

Holy Books
The Qur'an

Holy Symbol
Crescent and star

Quick Reference: Christianity

Worldwide distribution

Christianity is the world's largest religious group. There are around 2.2 billion Christians, which means that roughly one-third of the world's population follows this faith. Christians can be found living in every country of the world. About 37 percent of all Christians live in North or South America, while 26 percent live in Europe. In sub-Saharan Africa, about 24 percent of the population is Christian, while 13 percent of Asians or Pacific Islanders are Christian. The number of Christians is growing rapidly in both Africa and Asia, while the number of Christians is actually declining in Europe and North America.

There are thousands of different Christian groups or sects. About half of all Christians are Roman Catholic. The various Protestant denominations—such as Lutherans, Presbyterians, Methodists, Baptists, and the like—make up about 37 percent of the total. Orthodox Christians comprise 12 percent of Christians worldwide.

The United States is the country with the highest number of Christians, around 250 million (almost 80 percent of the U.S. population). Brazil is home to 175 million Christians, 90 percent of the population. Both Mexico and Russia are home to more than 100 million Christians. Nigeria has the largest

Christian population in sub-Saharan Africa with about 80 million Christians, roughly half of that country's population. The Philippines, with over 87 million Christians, are the largest population in Asia.

Branches of Christianity

For about 1,000 years there was only one Christian Church, but over time differences between the believers caused a division, or schism. The Church was divided into Roman Catholic and Eastern Orthodox branches in 1054 CE.

The Roman Catholic Church has its headquarters in the Vatican in Rome, and is headed by the pope, who is believed to be the successor to the Apostle Peter. Eastern Orthodox churches are divided into fourteen self-governing churches according to geographical region, such as the Russian Orthodox, Greek Orthodox, or Syrian Orthodox. The Eastern Orthodox churches are headed by a patriarch and a council of bishops.

Protestant churches broke away from the Roman Catholic Church during the Reformation of the sixteenth century. These churches do not accept the authority of the pope, and prefer to focus more on the Bible and less on rituals and apostolic traditions.

During the early twentieth century, the Pentecostal movement emerged in African-American communities. Pentecostals believe the Holy Spirit of God gives them power to heal and preach the Gospels. They are noted for their powerful singing and emotional services.

The Cathedral of Christ the Savior in Moscow is the largest Russian Orthodox church in the world. It was built after the collapse of the Soviet Union, on the site of an earlier church with the same name.

Christianity Timeline

c. 4 BCE   Birth of Jesus.

c. 29 CE   Crucifixion of Jesus.

50   At the Council of Jerusalem, Christian leaders agree that non-Jewish Christians do not need to follow Jewish laws related to diet or circumcision.

60–100   The four Gospels probably written.

c. 62   Death of Peter, Jesus's leading disciple and first Bishop of Rome.

c. 65   Death of St Paul.

64–312   Period of persecution of Christians by Romans after fire destroys part of Rome. Christians blamed.

70   Destruction of the Temple in Jerusalem.

84   Christians excluded from synagogues.

c. 200   Arrival of Christianity in Britain; development of Celtic Christianity.

312   The Emperor Constantine declares Christianity to be a legal religion in the Roman Empire; Christians begin church building.

325   Council of Nicaea.

382	Contents of the Christian Bible agreed.
c. 540	Benedict draws up rule for monastic movement.
597	Augustine arrives in Britain 'to bring English people back to Christianity'. Beginning of struggle between Roman and Celtic forms of Christianity.
1054	Separation of Roman Catholic Church from Orthodox Churches of the East.
1096	First Crusade begins to recapture Christian sites in Palestine from Muslims.
1170	Thomas Becket, Archbishop of Canterbury, is murdered in Canterbury Cathedral.
1209	Francis of Assisi founds Franciscan Order of monks.
1215	Dominican Order of monks founded by Dominic.
1517	Martin Luther posts his 95 Theses on church door in Wittenberg, heralding the start of the Reformation.
1534	Act of Supremacy recognizes Henry VIII as Head of English Church.
1536	John Calvin publishes his *Institutes*.
1611	King James I Authorized Version of the Bible is published.
1633	Mayflower sails to America to found colony guaranteeing religious freedom.
1642	George Fox starts the Religious Society of Friends (Quakers).

1738	John and Charles Wesley found the Methodist movement.
1822	Joseph Smith reports receiving visions, leading to the establishment of the Latter Day Saints Church (Mormons).
1868–70	First Vatican Council passes decree of Papal infallibility.
1878	Salvation Army founded by William Booth.
1910	Ecumenical beginnings of Christian Churches at Edinburgh Missionary Conference.
1948	Foundation of World Council of Churches; Roman Catholic nun Mother Teresa founds Order of the Missionaries of Charity.
1960	John F. Kennedy is the first Roman Catholic to be voted president of the United States.
1962–65	Second Vatican Council brings major changes to the Roman Catholic Church, such as allowing mass to be conducted in local languages, rather than in Latin.
1978	John Paul II becomes Roman Catholic pontiff. During his long papacy, he would help to end Communism in Europe and improved relations between the Catholic Church and other Christian churches, as well as with Muslim and Jewish organizations.
1986	Desmond Tutu becomes Anglican Archbishop of South Africa. He becomes an

outspoken leader in the anti-apartheid movement within that country.

2003   The Episcopal Church in the United States elects an openly gay priest, Gene Robinson, as bishop of the Diocese of New Hampshire. The controversial election leads to a schism in the church.

2005   Pope Benedict XVI is elected after the death of Pope John Paul II.

2007   The Creation Museum opens in Kentucky, United States; the Russian Orthodox Church is reunified after 80 years of schism.

2008   In December, the Vatican hosts a conference involving the Pontifical Council for Interfaith Dialogue and the World Islamic Call Society.

2009   August 21- The Minneapolis Churchwide Assembly of the ELCA passes four ministry policy resolutions that will permit clergy in committed homosexual partnerships to be rostered leaders within the ELCA.

2013   Pope Benedict resigns, and is succeeded by Pope Francis, an Argentinean who is the first non-European elected pope since the eighth century.

Series Glossary of Key Terms

afterlife—a term that refers to a continuation of existence beyond the natural world, or after death.

BCE and CE—alternatives to the traditional Western designation of calendar eras, which used the birth of Jesus as a dividing line. BCE stands for "Before the Common Era," and is equivalent to BC ("Before Christ"). Dates labeled CE, or "Common Era," are equivalent to *Anno Domini* (AD, or "the Year of Our Lord").

chant—the rhythmic speaking or singing of words or sounds, intended to convey emotion in worship or to express the chanter's spiritual side. Chants can be conducted either on a single pitch or with a simple melody involving a limited set of notes, and often include a great deal of repetition.

creation—the beginnings of humanity, earth, life, and the universe. According to most religions, creation was a deliberate act by a supreme being.

deity (or god)—a supernatural being, usually considered to have significant power. Deities/gods are worshiped and considered sacred by human beings. Some deities are believed to control time and fate, to be the ultimate judges of human worth and behavior, and to be the designers and creators of the Earth or the universe. Others are believed to control natural phenomena, such as lightning, floods, and storms. They can assume a variety of forms, but are frequently depicted as having human or animal form, as well as specific personalities and characteristics.

hymn—a song specifically written as a song of praise, adoration or prayer, typically addressed to a god or deity.

miracle—according to many religions, a miracle is an unusual example of divine intervention in the universe by a god or deity, often one in which natural laws are overruled, suspended, or modified.

prayer—an effort to communicate with a deity or god, or another form of spiritual entity. Prayers are usually intended to offer praise, to make a request, or simply to express the person's thoughts and emotions.

prophecy—the prediction of future events, thanks to either direct or indirect communication with a deity or god. The term prophecy is also used to describe the revelation of divine will.

religion—a system of belief concerning the supernatural, sacred, or divine; and the moral codes, practices, values, institutions and rituals associated with such belief. There are many different religions in the world today.

ritual—a formal, predetermined set of symbolic actions generally performed in a particular environment at a regular, recurring interval. The actions that make up a ritual often include, but are not limited to, such things as recitation, singing, group processions, repetitive dance, and manipulation of sacred objects. The general purpose of rituals is to engage a group of people in unified worship, in order to strengthen their communal bonds.

saint—a term that refers to someone who is considered to be exceptionally virtuous and holy. It can be applied to both the living and the dead and is an acceptable term in most of the world's popular religions. A saint is held up as an example of how all other members of the religious community should act.

worship—refers to specific acts of religious praise, honor, or devotion, typically directed to a supernatural being such as a deity or god. Typical acts of worship include prayer, sacrifice, rituals, meditation, holidays and festivals, pilgrimages, hymns or psalms, the construction of temples or shrines, and the creation of idols that represent the deity.

Organizations to Contact

Association of Christian Schools
731 Chapel Hills Drive
Colorado Springs, CO 80920
Phone: (719) 528.6906
Fax: (719) 531.0631
Email: press@acsi.org
Website: www.acsi.org

Catholic Charities USA
2050 Ballenger Ave Suite 400
Alexandria, VA 22314
Phone: (703) 549-1390
Fax: 703-549-1656
Email: info@catholiccharitiesusa.org
Website: https://catholiccharitiesusa.org

Christian Coalition of America
PO Box 37030
Washington, DC 20013
Phone (202) 479-6900
Website: www.cc.org

Food for the Hungry
1224 E. Washington Street
Phoenix, AZ 85034-1102
Phone: (800) 248-6437
Email: hunger@fh.org
Website: www.fh.org

Moody Bible Institute
820 N. LaSalle Blvd.
Chicago, IL 60610
Phone: (800) DL-MOODY
Website: www.moody.edu

Promise Keepers
P.O. Box 11798
Denver, CO 80211
Phone: (866) 776-6473.
Website: http://promisekeepers.org

Samaritan's Purse
PO Box 3000
Boone, NC 28607
Phone: (828) 262-1980.
Fax (828) 266-1056
Website: www.samaritanspurse.org

World Vision
P.O. Box 9716
Federal Way, WA 98063
Phone: (888) 511-6548
Website: www.worldvision.org

Further Reading

Bowker, John. *World Religions: The Great Faiths Explored and Explained*. London: Dorling Kindersley Ltd., 2006.

Levenson, Jon. D. *Inheriting Abraham: The Legacy of the Patriarch in Judaism, Christianity, and Islam*. Princeton, N.J.: Princeton University Press, 2014.

Mansfield, Peter. *A History of the Middle East*. 4th ed. revised and updated by Nicholas Pelham. New York: Penguin Books, 2013.

McDermott, Gerald R. *World Religions: An Indispensable Introduction*. Nashville, Tenn.: Thomas Nelson, 2011.

Schafer, Peter. *The Jewish Jesus: How Judaism and Christianity Shaped Each Other*. Princeton, N.J.: Princeton University Press, 2012.

Smith, Huston. *The World's Religions*. New York: HarperCollins, 2009.

Wenisch, Fritz. *Judaism, Christianity, and Islam: Differences, Commonalities, and Community*. 2nd ed. San Diego: Cognella Academic Publishing, 2014.

Internet Resources

www.christianity.com
Learn all about Christianity at Christianity.com with articles and videos focused on the life of Jesus Christ, the Christian church, and Christian living for families.

www.christianitytoday.com
Website of Christianity Today, a magazine for evangelical Christians that features articles on Christian topics.

www.bbc.co.uk/religion/religions/christianity
This page from the British Broadcasting Company (BBC) provides information about Christian beliefs, customs, history, and ethics.

www.pewresearch.org/topics/christians-and-christianity
This page run by the Pew Research Center provides links to polls and articles about the opinions and attitudes of Christians in the United States and other countries.

www.cia.gov/library/publications/the-world-factbook
The CIA World Factbook is a convenient source of basic information about any country in the world. This site includes links to a page on each country with religious, geographic, demographic, economic, and governmental data.

www.biblegateway.com

Bible Gateway is a searchable database of the Old and New Testaments of the Bible. Various translations are available, and commentaries and notes are hyperlinked to specific Bible verses of interest.

www.sacred-texts.com

The Internet Sacred Text Archive has an enormous repository of electronic texts about religion, mythology, legends and folklore, and occult and esoteric topics. Texts related to Christianity include the writings of the early church fathers, Gnostic texts, and works by such important figures as Thomas Aquinas and Francis of Assisi.

www.newadvent.org/cathen/

The Catholic Encyclopedia, which was originally published early in the 20th century, is a searchable database of articles about important people and events in the history of Christianity.

Index

Numbers in ***bold italics*** refer to captions.

27–30, 33, 75–76
as the Messiah, 14, 26, 29, 43,
47
and miracles, 11–12, 22, 24, 25,
28
and parables, 8, 9–10
resurrection of, 8, *9*, 13–14,
34–37, 43, 63, 75
teachings of, 9–13, 15, 24–27,
29, 35–37, 39, 40, 45, 79, 82
See also Christianity
John (apostle), 30, 35, 40, 47
John (Gospel author), 36, 40, 41
John the Baptist, 24, *25*, 35
Judah, 20, 21
Judaism, 10, 11, 29–30, 40, 41, 42
and early Christianity, 41,
42–46
history of, 17–22, 24
and Jesus Christ, 9, 12–13,
24–30, 33–35
and Passover, 27–28, 29, 30, 76
See also Christianity
Judas, 30
Judea, 22, 29, 46

Last Rites (sacrament), 74
See also sacraments
"laying on of hands," 74
See also Healing (sacrament)
Lent, 64, 75
Licinius, 51
Luke (Gospel author), 40, 41
Luther, Martin, 60, *62*
Lutheran churches, 13, *61*, 62, 84,
86, 89
See also Protestant churches

Marcus Aurelius, 49
Mark (Gospel author), 40, 41
marriage, 64, 69, 72–73, 85
See also sacraments
martyrdom, *44*, 47, *48*, 49

Matthew (Gospel author), 40, 41,
47
Methodist church, 13, *61*, 62, 89
See also Protestant churches
miracles, 8, 11–12, 22, 24, 25, 28,
42
Moses, 17–18, *20*, 21, 27, 28, 40
Mother Teresa, *80*, 81

Nero, 49, 57
New Testament, 8, *24*, 39–41, 66
See also Bible
Nicene creed, 53, 54, 63

Old Testament, 8, 19, 39–40, 66,
84–85
See also Bible
Ordination, 64, 69, 73, 82, 86
See also sacraments
Orthodox church, 13, *49, 58*, 60,
74, 84, 86, 95
and church services, 66, 67–68
and sacraments, 64, 69, 70

parables, 8, 9–10
Passover, 27–28, 29, 30, 76
Paul, 40, 42, 43–45, 47, 49, 57
as Saul of Tarsus, 42–43
Pentecostal movement, 62–63, 66,
96
Peter, 30, 35, 40, 41, 42, *44*, 47, 49,
57–58, 82, 84, 96
Pontius Pilate, 30, *31*, 33
popes, 38, *57*, 58, 59, 89, 96
Presbyterian church, *61*, 62, 84, 86,
89
See also Protestant churches
prophets, 16, 21–22, 40
Protestant churches, 13, *39, 61*, 62,
78, 86, 95, 96
and church services, 66, 68–69
and denominations, *61*, 62–63
and sacraments, 64, 69, 70, 74

and women clergy, 84
Protestant Reformation, 60, 62, 96

Religious Society of Friends
   (Quakers), 62
research projects, 15, 37, 63, 77, 91
resurrection, 8, *9*, 13–14, 34–37,
   43, 63, 75
   See also Jesus Christ
Robinson, Gene, 86
Roman Catholic church, *7*, 13, *39,
   53, 57*, 62, 84, 86, 95, 96
   and abortion, 86–87
   and church services, 66, 67–68
   and contraception, 87–88
   and Mary, *24*
   origins of the, 60
   and popes, 38, *57*, 58, 59, 89, 96
   and sacraments, 64, 69–72,
      73–74
   and Ten Commandments, 19
Roman Empire, 22, 26
   and Christianity as state reli-
      gion, 56–60
   division of the, 49–51, 55–59
   and Jewish revolts, 29, 30, *31*
   and legalization of Christianity,
      50–53, 55
   and persecution of Christians,
      42, 46, 49, 51
   and spread of Christianity,

45–46, *50*, 51, 55
Rome, 46, 47, 51, 56, 57–59, 96
   decline of, 59–60
   See also Roman Empire

sacraments, 64, 69–74
sacred tradition, 78, 80
Sanhedrin, 29–30, 42
Saul of Tarsus, 42–43
   See also Paul
services, church, 65–69, *85*
Simon. *See* Peter
Solomon, 20
Stephen, 42

Ten Commandments, 18, 19, 27
   See also commandments
Tertullian, 49
Tetrarchy, 50
   See also Roman Empire
Trinity, 14, 38, 52

Valerian, 49

"The Way," 39
   See also Christianity
women clergy, 82, 84
worship services. *See* services,
   church

Yeshua. *See* Jesus Christ

About the Author

Aaron Bowen is a graduate of St. Charles Borromeo Seminary outside of Philadelphia. This is his first book for young people.